Molded By Life

AF624651

Sanni Tju

BookLeaf Publishing

Presentation by *BookLeaf Publishing*

Web: www.bookleafpub.com

E-mail: info@bookleafpub.com

ISBN: 9789357211895

First edition 2023

Looks can be deceiving

Don't judge the book by its cover
Looks can be deceiving
Things may not be what it appears
Don't always trust what you see

You see what I appear to be
You only see what I choose to show
There are two sides to every coin
There is a story behind the smile
You see my smile, but you don't know my tears
Don't be jealous, but be content
Neighbour's grass is not always greener

Create a world free of judgment
Don't judge unless you walk in my shoes
Don't assume, but be curious
Listen and seek to understand
Be kind because you don't know what others are going through
Your smile and being might be what they need

Opportunity

Opportunity is knocking, will you open it?
Opportunity is calling, will you answer it?
Opportunity is whispering in your ears, will you hear it?
Opportunity is flying in front of your eyes, will you grab it?

Grab the opportunity when it comes
Nothing is more expensive than missed opportunities
Opportunity is nowhere
Opportunity is now here

Disguised as hard work
Disguised as challenges
Disguised as failure
Opportunity is everywhere

The Precious Gift of Life

Life is God's given gift, a precious gift
Open it, cherish it, and make it count
But nothing is eternity
And can be taken away

Don't take life for granted
It is too precious, too unpredictable, and too short
Be grateful for what you have and cherish them
Tell someone you care that you love them

Don't take life for granted
It can change in a blink of an eye
One moment you are happy, one moment you are sad
One moment you are breathing, then one moment it's your last breath
One moment there is arrival, one moment time for departure

Don't take life for granted
It might be your last chance
And once taken away
There is no way to get it back

Forgive often, love with all your heart
Because life is truly a precious gift
Live each day as if it was your last

Happy Birthday

Today is a special day for an extraordinary
person
Who deserves the best that each day can bring
Another number is attached to you
Age is just a number, but who's counting?

Whatever your number is, you're forever
youthful
Whatever your number is, you're as beautiful as
ever
Whatever your number is, I love you
Whatever your number is, I'm grateful to you

Influential person in my life
The lessons that you taught
The legacy you've imprinted
You are a gem, a treasure
Forever in my heart

Wishing you a very Happy Birthday
May your day be as extraordinary as you are
Stay healthy and stay happy
Forever love, your daughter

Eyes Are The Windows To The Soul

You can wear masks to hide your pain
You can smile and pretend all are good
But you can't hide from me
You have drawn me into your world

Your eyes speak volumes,
When I see your eyes, I see all of you
When I see your eyes, I see your pain
When I see your eyes, I see your fear
When I see your eyes, I see your sadness

Unmask your mask, and be yourself
No explanation is needed, don't say a word
Lean on me and let me hug
You are safe, as I will always protect you

Hope

When you can't find the sunshine
Be the sun to lighten up someone's life
Be the moon to brighten in the darkest hour
Be the rainbow in someone's cloud
Whatever it is, be something for someone
You are needed, you are important
Soon enough, you will hear hope
Singing the tune without words
Whispering to remind you to keep going
Waking up the heroes inside you
Open your heart and listen
Follow the anchor of your soul
Shake your body, shake your fears and doubts,
and dance

Reflection Of The Year

Greeted the year with excitement
Last year was tough, but this year will be the best year ever
Out with the old, in with the new
A book with 365 blank pages for us to fill

Planning for the whole year
Writing down resolutions for the year
Want to do this, want to do that
This year will be MY year

But the year has its mind, and reality has spoken
Things don't go according to plan
Take us by surprise, not feeling prepared
Filled with fear, panic, and disappointment

Questioning why this is happening
The beautiful vision suddenly gone
With a sudden abrupt change
Gut-wrenching

Learn to stop and rest, an opportunity to recharge
Learn to appreciate everything and everyone
Learn to love and be kind to one another

Learn to enjoy the journey along the way

As we are about to say goodbye to this year
Take a 360-degree tour of the year
Reflect and take the lessons that the year brings
The thought of how do I go through this,
But guess what? We made it through the year.

Welcoming the new year with the same
excitement
And start fresh with yet another blank 365 pages

Extra

Being good is ordinary
Being great is extraordinary
The difference between good ad great is the
extra miles.

Taking two steps forward instead of one
Sometimes three steps backward instead of two
Take chances and do what others are afraid to do

It comes with patience and sacrifices,
Expect temptations and fears to come
It's not easy, yet it's so worth it

Don't settle for only good,
You are born to be great
Just take that extra mile

Beauty In The Eye Of The Beholder

They say beauty is in the eye of the beholder
If you can't see beauty in yourself
See from the eyes of loved ones
So you can see what you can't see yourself
Hear from the voice and heart of the loved ones
Feel the vibration of the heart
They are trying to tell you that you are loved
Feel the vibration of the voice
They are trying to let you know
You are beautiful inside and out

Patience is virtue

When things are not according to plan
Just remember that good thing take time
Diamonds are molded not in one day
Flowers do not bloom in one day
Castle is built not in one day

Don't fight it, and don't rush it
What is yours will come at the right time
Enjoy the process along the way
Things will unfold in their own time

Patience is virtue
Because the best things in life
Are worth waiting for

The greatest gift

The greatest gift for self is life
Given by the creator above
To wake up in the morning
To be able to breathe

Life is a gift that keeps giving
It gives the ability to share the greatest gift with others
Whatever their situation at any one point in time

For someone who is blind, eyesight is the greatest gift
For someone who is deaf, hearing is the greatest gift
For someone who is mute, voice is the greatest gift
For someone who has no legs or arms, mobile legs or arms are the greatest gift

For someone who sees only black and grey, colors are the greatest gift
For someone who is lonely, friendship is the greatest gift
For someone who is angry or hates, love and peace are the greatest gift

For someone who is stuck, a way out is the greatest gift

For someone who is homeless, even a shelter is the greatest gift
For someone who is hungry, food is the greatest gift
For someone who is thirsty, water is the greatest gift

For someone who is having a bad day, a smile is the greatest gift
For someone who lost loved ones, time is the greatest gift
For someone who is tired, a break is the greatest gift
For someone who is sick, health is the greatest gift
For someone who is separated, news or phone calls are the greatest gift
For me, YOU are the greatest gift

I am abundantly blessed with the perfect gifts

Big Kids At Home

Remember when we were kids
Tell the same story over and over again
Ask the same question multiple times
Throw tantrums and are stubborn
Made a mess during mealtime

They listened to the same story,
Answered the same question multiple times
Listened to our frustration and gave us space to express our emotions
Clean up our mess during mealtime
Cared for us when we were sick
Lots of cuddling, hug, and I love you

Now they act like a kid,
And need a lot of help
Tell the same story over and over again
Ask the same question multiple times
Throwing tantrums and are stubborn
Making a mess during mealtime

It's our turn to care for them
Love them as they loved us when we were kids
Listen to the same story over and over again
Answer the same question multiple times

Listen to their frustration and give them space to express their emotions
Clean up their mess during mealtime
Care for them when they are sick
Lots of cuddling, hug, and I love you

Love our parents as they loved us when we were kids

Time

I wish I can have had more time
To do the things that I need to do
I wish I can have had more time
To spend with the people that I love
I wish I could buy time
So I can do what my heart desire
I wish I could stop the time
To savor the precious moment
I wish...

I can't stop time,
Time keeps going with or without me
Can't buy extra time
Once lost, I can't get it back

I choose to be friends with time
I can appreciate the moment now
I can appreciate the people around me, not
taking them for granted
I can live life to the fullest, do what my heart
desire today
I can...

I appreciate time more than ever

Five Minutes

Do things consciously, even the mundane ones
Not for the sake of doing it
Take extra five minutes
Consciously aware as we are doing it

Shower consciously
Notice the water flowing through
Imagine the water flushing the tiredness, stress, and worry
Imagine the water cleansing the shame and guilt

Eat consciously
Being aware of what we put into our body
The colors, the texture, the warmth
Savor the burst of different flavors blending.

Breathe consciously
Focus on the breath
Create the space of void, and notice our thoughts
Notice as we inhale and exhale

Take an extra five minutes in everything we do
It may seem a little, but it makes a difference
Take an extra five for yourself, and the rest can wait

Because you are worth an additional five minutes

Friendship

Every friendship story is beautiful
But ours is my favorite

We crossed each other's paths
Arranged at the divine time
From stranger to friend to family
Connected not with blood but with soul
Separated not by distance or time

Fill my cup with joy and laughter
Fill my heart with love and kindness
Life becomes fuller and more beautiful

Blessed with this precious gift called friendship
I must have done something right
When He arranged our path to cross
Thank you for being part of my life

Firsts

When was the last time you did things for the first time?
Kids get excited about anything and everything
They look at the world in awe and wonder
They see the world as a playground
Trying things the first time, knowing no boundaries or fear
Exploring while having fun along the way

Remember those "first" life milestones
The first word, first walk, the first talk
First time working, getting married, and getting a house
And many more

Mixed emotions blended
Doubt and fear will come up because of the unknown
But it will fill your heart with excitement and joy
Excited to see what life will unfold

Amplify the excitement, and quieten the doubt and fear

Open your mind and see the world as a playground
Get comfortable with being sucked the first time
Keep going until you get better at it

Life is an exploration. There's so much to explore in the world
There will be many firsts, and the choice is yours to make
Be proud of doing things the first time
Many are too afraid to try, missing out on the joy of trying things.

Giant Classroom

Nature is a giant classroom to be explored
Full of magic and adventure that never ends
Life is the only pass to attend the classroom
Everything in nature teaches us something
Ready to teach those who want to learn

We are students of nature,
We learn through experiment and adventure
Learning from one another
While having fun along the way

The sun teaches us how to shine brightly
The trees teach us to stay rooted and flexible
The water teaches us about ebb and flow
The moon and the stars teach us that there is
light in the darkness.

We are lifelong learners,
Attend the classroom with an open mind and
curiosity
Observe the small details of nature
And the lessons it tries to teach

Say good morning as we arrive at the school
Respect one another

Be kind to one another
What do we learn today?

Note To Self

Dear self,

Stop comparing yourself with anyone,
With whom are you competing?
What is the prize if you win or they win?
What competition are you joining?
Who is the judge? What is the standard?

You are comparing an apple and an orange
Never was, never is, and never will be the same
You are at the perfect time and perfect place
You are doing the best with what you know

Life is not a competition.
Stop worrying that you are not going as fast as others
You are making progress and in the right direction
Look at how far you've come
Be proud and celebrate

Be

Be curious, for we don't know what we don't know,
Be objective, as there are always two sides to the coin
Be open-minded, welcome opportunities
Be free, releasing the fear
Be excited for the best is yet to come
Be humble, keep your feet on the ground
Be a dreamer, look up to the sky, and dream

Destination Map

Life is a journey to a destination without a printed map
We created the map as we go

Making choices throughout the day
Turn left, turn right, or go straight
Every choice leads us to another path
Sometimes we don't know where the path will bring us
Then we realize we took a wrong turn
That is called a mistake

We try to find a U-turn called second chances
Remember not to take that path again
That is a lesson learned
In the end, it will always bring us to the destination.

Our journey will become a map,
For others going to the same destination
That is called a legacy
So don't be afraid to make mistakes

Love

Love is in the air
Love from you
Love from me
Together we are creating a loving world

Love one another
Care for one another
Sharing the love
Spreading the love
What a loving world it is

Love is blind
Love is red even when it's black
Love is sweet even when it's sour
Love is beautiful even when it is ugly
Love is joyful, but sometimes it is hurtful
Love is blind until your eyes opened
Love anyway as you are love and come from a
place of love

www.ingramcontent.com/pod-product-compliance
Lightning Source LLC
Chambersburg PA
CBHW051758130826
49812CB00033B/1193
* 9 7 8 9 3 5 7 2 1 1 8 9 5 *